THE MYSTERY OF THE TITANIC

The Titanic

A HISTORICAL INVESTIGATION FOR KIDS

KELLY MILNER HALLS

Illustrated by Joanne Lew-Vriethoff

ROCKRIDGE
PRESS

Interior and Cover Designer: Rachel Haeseker
Art Producer: Sue Bischofberger
Editor: Laura Apperson
Production Editor: Sigi Nacson
Production Manager: Holly Haydash

Illustration © 2020 Joanne Lew-Vriethoff
Photography © New York Public Library/Science Source, cover and pp. ii, 27, 29, and 51; courtesy of George Grantham Bain Collection/Library of Congress, cover and pp. vi, xii, 4, 52; Patrick Landmann/Science Source, pp. ii and 86; Historic Collection/Alamy Stock Photo, p. 31; courtesy of Library of Congress/2002721378, pp. 53 and 90; PJF Military Collection/Alamy Stock Photo, p. 54; Ralph White/Getty Images, pp. 54 and 83; Christopher W. Morrow/Science Source, p. 62; NG Images/Alamy Stock Photo, p. 65
Author photo courtesy of Roxyanne Young

ISBN: Print 978-1-64739-877-4 | Ebook 978-1-64739-555-1
R0

This book is dedicated to my grandmother's aunt, who died in the sinking of the *Lusitania*, a ship that helped inspire the *Titanic*. May the lives lost at sea be forever remembered.

CONTENTS

INTRODUCTION

Ships moved the world in the early 1900s. And none had more magic than the RMS *Titanic*.

Brought to life by the British shipping company White Star Line and the Harland and Wolff **shipyard** in Ireland, it was the largest, most beautiful ocean liner of its time. With a **hull** made of huge steel plates and three million iron and steel **rivets**, it measured 882 feet, 9 inches long and weighed 46,328 tons.

The *Titanic*'s first-class **staterooms** were **luxurious**. Many elements of its first-class gathering spaces were modeled after the French palace of Versailles.

When the ship set sail on April 10, 1912, it carried the pride of the 14,000 Irishmen who had built it, not to mention the hopes and dreams of its passengers and crew members. Many of those hopes and dreams soon died at sea.

How did this tragedy unfold? Why did it happen? What mysteries sank to the bottom of the ocean? This book will answer those questions in two sections.

Part 1 will take you on that ill-fated voyage. You will stroll the open-air decks with the wealthy and share a hearty meal with the second- and third-class passengers who scrimped and saved for a once-in-a-lifetime adventure—and who left everything behind in hope of a better life in America.

As the ship cruises the calm ocean at a speedy 21 **knots**, you'll notice bits of ice appear in the water as the sun goes down. You'll hear the warning cries, "Iceberg ahead!" You'll feel the ship scrape against the rock-hard ice.

When the **bow** starts to dip into the frosty Atlantic, you'll hope for a seat on a lifeboat as the string quartet plays on. They'll be playing music to inspire hope. They'll be playing songs to slow the panic. But will they survive?

As you sail through the book, watch out for our detective, who will pop up every time there is a hidden clue on a page—a bit of information sure to help unravel the secrets of the *Titanic*. Some of the clues might be hard to find and others might only make sense later on. We'll work together to uncover the mystery of the *Titanic*.

Part 2 of this book will reveal why the *Titanic* sank and how it was rediscovered. What did those clues tell us about this famous disaster? Read on to find out.

FUN FACT: RMS?

The "RMS" in RMS *Titanic* stands for "Royal Mail Ship."
The *Titanic* carried about 3,243 bags of mail. Each bag
held more than 2,000 letters and packages.

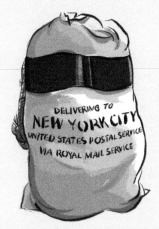

The Royal Mail Ship *Titanic* was set to
deliver mail to New York City.

THE TITANIC

When they bought tickets to cruise on the luxury liner *Titanic*, passengers believed they were about to sail from England to America on an unsinkable ship. White Star Line, the company that built the boat, never actually called the ship "unsinkable" in advertisements, but the newspapers did. *Why deny something that might help sell staterooms?* the company owners thought. So, they didn't correct what the newspapers printed.

After all, the *Titanic* was one of the safest ships of its time, equipped with state-of-the-art technology including top-notch wireless radio equipment, all the luxury money could buy, and every lifeboat required by law. What harm could the headlines do?

But accidents happen, and the fact that the bow of the massive ship was soon dipping into the Atlantic proved the newspapers were mistaken. How could things go so horribly wrong? How could so many people certain they were on an unsinkable ship wind up dying in a dark, frosty ocean long before dawn?

CHAPTER 1

Building the Titanic

Launch of a Dream

It all started in 1907 at the grand Downshire House in London, England.

Lord William Pirrie and his wife, Margaret, invited J. Bruce Ismay and his wife, Florence, to their home for dinner. Pirrie ran the Harland and Wolff shipyard in Belfast, Ireland, which made some of the finest ships in Europe. Ismay ran the White Star Line, one of Britain's most successful shipping companies. They bought the ships that Pirrie made.

White Star's main competitor, the Cunard Line, had just introduced two new sister ships, the *Lusitania* and the *Mauretania*. They were big and they were fast. Both had four steam **turbine** engines that turned four powerful propellers. With 70,000 horsepower in motion, they could reach a speed of 27 knots, or around 31 miles per hour. They could sail across the Atlantic, from London to New York City, in just under five days.

Ismay feared the Cunard ships would leave White Star in the dust. But Pirrie had a plan.

White Star would create brand-new sisters of its own, the *Olympic* and the *Titanic*. The ships would be 883 feet long, nearly 100 feet longer than Cunard's duo. Their three propeller engines would only be able to muster 22 knots at 40,000 horsepower, adding a full day to their Atlantic crossing time. But White Star had an ace up its sleeve.

DEEP DIVE: WHAT IS HORSEPOWER?

In 1702, Thomas Savery was among the first to compare the power of the newly created steam engine to the power of a horse. Engines were about to replace workhorses, so it made sense. About 70 years later, engineer James Watt took that comparison a little further. He determined that a horse could turn a mill wheel 144 times in an hour, using 180 pounds of muscle. That, he said, was 1 horsepower. The *Titanic*'s engines ran at 40,000 horsepower, burning hundreds of tons of coal—not hay or grain.

What the *Olympic* and the *Titanic* lacked in horsepower, they would make up for in sheer luxury. Passengers would board a pair of floating palaces so lovely, the extra 24 hours would be a bonus, not a disappointment.

The two men shook hands. They made a gentleman's agreement to build the ships in four to five years for the cost of materials plus a 3 percent profit. And with that, the race was on.

The *Titanic* and her twin sister, the *Olympic*, were built at Harland and Wolff, side by side.

THE TITANIC'S DESIGNERS

Although Thomas Andrews is often called the *Titanic*'s designer, another man, named Alexander Carlisle, was the first designer for the *Titanic* and the *Olympic*. As the company's chief naval architect, Carlisle

had already designed other noteworthy ships.

The giant sister ships were his new challenge. And for three years, he worked to bring Pirrie's dream to life. But in the summer of 1910, Carlisle suddenly left Harland and Wolff forever, just as the *Titanic* was being framed.

Some say he left after an argument with Pirrie about lifeboats. Carlisle insisted on 48 lifeboats for each of the sisters—enough to seat every passenger aboard. Pirrie and Ismay settled for what the **Board of Trade** laws required—16 lifeboats, with an extra 4 collapsible lifeboats as a compromise.

Others say Carlisle was tired of violent shipyard battles over religion and politics. After Carlisle retired, Pirrie asked his nephew Thomas Andrews to take Carlisle's place. Andrews was only 37 years old, but he was ready for the job.

FUN FACT: LIFEBOATS BY THE NUMBERS

When she left Europe, the *Titanic* carried:

- One 25-foot-long wooden **cutter** that could carry 40 people
- One 23-foot-long wooden cutter that could carry 40 people
- Fourteen 30-foot-long wooden lifeboats that could each carry 65 people
- 4 collapsible lifeboats that could each carry 47 people

A total of 1,178 people could have been saved, if all of the boats had been full.

Passengers and crew totaled 2,233 souls.

THE BUILD

Before construction could begin, the Harland and Wolff shipyard had to be rebuilt to make room for the massive new projects.

Three of its original **slipways**—boat ramps for building and launching ocean liners—were replaced with two bigger slipways to cradle the *Olympic* and *Titanic* as they came to life. A massive construction frame called a **gantry** was then raised to box in each project. The giant structure required 6,000 tons of steel from Scotland and rose more than 228 feet in the air.

Mobile cranes were hung from the gantry. Custom-made to move easily, they could reach every part of the ships. A giant steel spine called a **keel** was built for each ship to support its frame and hull. Removable wooden beams rested beneath. They would be knocked away on the day the ships were ready to launch into the water.

Construction on the *Olympic* began on December 16, 1908. Work on the *Titanic* started three months later. More than 14,000 men—**fitters**, carpenters, **riveters, catchers,** and other skilled craftsmen—built the sister ships at the same time. It was a huge job.

For nine hours a day, six days a week, dedicated Irishmen took great pride in their hard work. They were the best of their trade, and yet most earned only 2 **pounds** a week for their enormous efforts. What would two 1908 British pounds be worth today? Just 242 pounds in the United Kingdom, or about $324 in the United States.

Bathroom breaks were known as "the Minutes," because a foreman kept track of how much time they took. Each man was given 7 minutes a day to answer the call of nature. But a 45-minute dinner break gave them more time to eat and reflect.

On Sunday, the workers' only day off, the men would go to church and then bring their families to see the ships' progress.

After a year, the *Titanic* skeleton was complete, and it was time to apply the ship's outer skin—its hull. One by one, the men attached 2,000 steel plates, each at least 30 feet long and 6 feet wide, to the *Titanic*'s shell. Each plate was at least 1 inch thick and weighed about 3 tons. Both steel and **wrought iron** rivets were used to piece together the steel plates of the *Titanic*'s hull. Steel was more expensive and stronger, so those rivets were used on the ship's central hull. Wrought iron rivets were less expensive, so they were used on the ship's bow and **stern**—its front and back.

Red-hot rivets of iron and steel came straight from the fire to the catcher's metal tongs. It was his job to rush them to the riveters before they could cool. The heat-fired rivets acted like staples, locking the plates in place. But the hull was too curved to allow them to use bulky machines to apply the rivets. So the men had to apply them by hand. More than 1,500 tons of flaming metal stitches were pounded into place.

Rivets held the massive metal plates of the *Titanic*'s hull in place. This tool carried the red-hot metal rivets to the plates.

Although most of the workers collected 2 pounds a week, the riveters were paid by the rivet. The faster they worked, the more money they took home. But speed can mean danger.

EIGHT MEN DIED

Harland and Wolff planned for the death of 1 worker for every 100,000 pounds spent on building a ship. They expected 15 would perish building the *Titanic*. But only 8 men died. The first—15-year-old rivet catcher Samuel Joseph Scott—fell on April 20, 1910, trying to deliver a red-hot rivet he was holding with a pair of tongs to the men who would pound it into place. He was buried in Belfast City Cemetery. He didn't receive a headstone until August 2011.

With the hull complete, the engines were next: 29 **boilers** fed by 159 coal-burning furnaces were carefully designed to fit into 16 compartments. Each would burn 600 tons of coal every day the ship was in service. The compartments would be **watertight** thanks to automatic steel doors that would close at the first sign of danger.

If one, two, three, or even four of the compart-ments took on water, the *Titanic* would still not sink. The technology was brand-new, and it was the pride of the shipyard.

The steam produced by the coal furnaces in each compartment would run three powerful engines—two **reciprocal engines** on either side of the ship that

The *Titanic*'s propellers were four times the height of an average man.

could **throttle** her forward or backward, and one turbine engine in the center that could power forward only. Each of the three bronze propellers was four times the height of an average man.

On launch day, the *Titanic*'s shell weighed about 24,000 tons. Freshly painted black, red, and white, she shined like a new penny.

As the workmen knocked away the wooden planks that had shored her up as she was built, the *Titanic* began to settle into her slipway. Because she was carefully coated with 22 tons of liquid soap and train oil, she finally began to slide—screaming and scraping toward the water. Two triggers held her back at the last minute, waiting for the command to sound.

> ## Release the triggers.
> —Lord William Pirrie, head of Harland and Wolff

The *Titanic* gently slid backward into the water at a surprisingly swift 12 knots, "the speed of a trotting horse," one witness said. In just 62 seconds, she glided into the river Lagan. The biggest ship ever made was afloat. She was then towed to the Thompson dry dock, where she'd be **fitted** and turned into a luxury ship.

A dry dock is a seaside slip where ships can be parked afloat. Once the ship is in place, a gate is closed and the seawater is pumped out to allow for mechanical fittings and repairs near the water, but not in the water.

The *Titanic*'s outer shell was complete, but her engines, furnaces, boilers, propellers, plumbing, electrical circuits, and more still had to be installed. Also missing was her interior magic—the carpentry and design that would make her worthy of the very rich, along with ordinary passengers.

It was there that a team of carpenters, engineers, plumbers, electricians, and painters began the *Titanic*'s stunning transformation. They added her furnaces, boilers, and engines, as well as her propellers.

They fitted her with four 60-ton smokestacks called **funnels**, each rising a full 81.5 feet high above the *Titanic*'s highest deck. They were 22 feet around. Three spewed black smoke and **soot** that was produced by the ship's burning coal furnaces. That soot is why the funnels were six stories tall. White Star wanted to protect the *Titanic*'s passengers from being bathed in coal dust on deck.

The fourth funnel did not process coal exhaust. It helped with the *Titanic*'s ventilation, but it was largely installed because designers felt it made her look more powerful and majestic.

Only three of the *Titanic*'s funnels were real smokestacks.

FUN FACT: LADY SHIPS?

Why are British ships often seen as female, such as the "sisters" *Titanic* and *Olympic*? According to Europe's Imperial War Museums, ships of old were considered protective, like mothers or goddesses, at sea. So, they were described with feminine pronouns like "her" and "she." However, the German captain Ernst Lindemann called his World War II ship, the *Bismarck*, "him" and "he." These traditions continue today. But the shipping newspaper *Lloyd's Register of Ships* now takes a gender-neutral stand, calling ships "it."

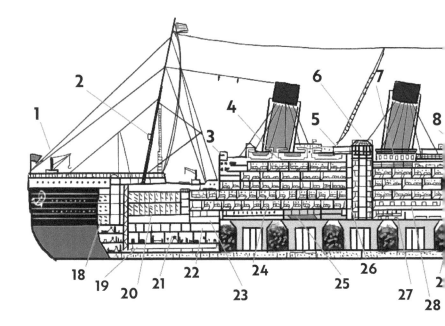

If you could look through the metal plates of the *Titanic*'s hull with X-ray vision, this is what you would see.

1. Cargo crane
2. Crow's nest
3. Bridge
4. Officers' quarters
5. Marconi Room
6. Forward Grand Staircase
7. Gymnasium
8. Compass platform
9. First-class staterooms
10. Maids and valets dining saloon
11. À la Carte restaurant
12. First-class smoking rooms
13. Second-class smoking rooms
14. Café Parisien
15. Second-class staterooms
16. Third-class smoking room
17. Stern bridge for docking
18. Crew quarters
19. Fireman's passage

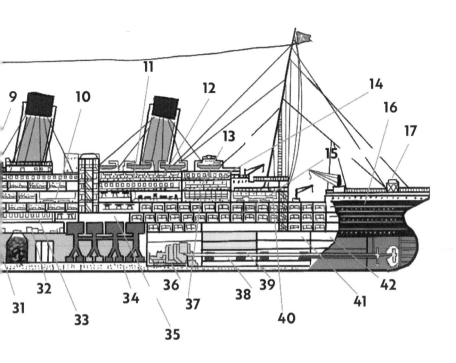

20. Third-class berths
21. Cargo berths
22. Post office
23. Squash court
24. First-class staterooms
25. Swimming pool and bath
26. First-class elevator
27. Turkish baths
28. First-class reception room
29. Boiler and coal bunker
30. Boilers
31. Third-class dining room
32. Third-class kitchen
33. First-class dining room
34. Reciprocating engines
35. Galley kitchen
36. Turbine engines
37. Library
38. Propeller shaft tunnel
39. Freshwater tanks
40. Second-class dining room
41. Refrigerated cargo
42. Third-class staterooms

INTERNAL BEAUTY

Ten passenger decks were fashioned from the finest pine flooring—the boat deck; the promenade deck; passenger decks B, C, D, E, F, and G; the orlop deck; and the tank top. Taking a brisk walk would never be a problem on the good ship *Titanic*.

The **forward** Grand Staircase was one of the *Titanic*'s most beautiful internal creations. It bridged seven full decks on the ship and welcomed first-class passengers to the **elegant** staterooms, walkways, lounges, and other special privileges reserved for the wealthiest travelers. All seven decks had to be constructed before the ship could sail.

When the craftsmen finished, the *Titanic* was the picture of **glamour** and perfection. She was solid and grand and admired by all who saw her. But the ship of dreams faced one final test.

> *I was thoroughly familiar with pretty well every type of ship afloat, but it took me 14 days before I could, with confidence, find my way from one part of the ship to another.*
>
> —Charles Lightoller, second officer of the *Titanic*

SEA TRIALS

Board of Trade representative Francis Carruthers had done more than 2,000 inspections on the *Titanic*, even before the ship slid into the Atlantic. But on the early morning of Monday, April 2, 1912—just eight days before the *Titanic* was set to begin her first **transatlantic** journey—Carruthers arrived to put her through her paces.

She had to pass her sea trials to prove she was safe enough to transport paying passengers.

By 6:00 a.m., a partial crew was in place—Captain E. J. Smith was on the bridge; 78 **stokers, greasers,** and firemen were in the engine rooms to feed the furnaces; and 41 others manned the ship's most important stations. For six hours, Carruthers tested every possible function on the massive ocean liner, and she did well.

Then she faced her greatest challenge. How quickly could she stop?

As the crew brought the *Titanic* to her full speed of 21 knots, Carruthers pulled out his **stopwatch** and ordered the ship to come to a halt. As the seconds ticked by, the crew wondered if she would make the grade.

She mastered the task. In just 850 yards, less than three times her own length, the *Titanic* went from 21 knots to dead in the water. Carruthers declared her seaworthy and signed a certificate good for a full year. The *Titanic* left Belfast at twelve noon that same day, with Thomas Andrews and his Guarantee Group—nine star employees at Harland and Wolff who had earned passage on her maiden voyage. They headed for Southampton, England—about 577 miles away—to pick up the bulk of the crew, passengers, and supplies. Soon, the *Titanic* would be bound for New York City.

The final cost was roughly $7.5 million. If she were reconstructed today, the price tag would be much higher, nearly $400 million.

FUN FACT: SISTER SLAMMED

E. J. Smith captained the *Titanic*, but he'd also captained her sister ship, the *Olympic*. Unfortunately, the *Olympic* had collided with the British cruiser HMS *Hawke* on September 20, 1911. The *Hawke*'s sharp-nosed bow had slammed into the **starboard**, or right, side of the *Olympic*, tearing two large holes in her hull. Two of her automatically sealed compartments were flooded, but she made it safely back to Belfast for repairs. The fact that she survived the accident gave people confidence that the *Titanic* would be safe, too.

CHAPTER 2

Life on the Titanic

The *Titanic* arrived in Southampton on April 3, 1912. She welcomed passengers and crew on April 10.

The week of April 3 was a flurry of activity. The *Titanic* needed coal to fuel its maiden voyage, and lots of it. But coal was increasingly difficult to find.

Coal miners in Britain were on strike. They refused to work until the coal companies agreed to give them more money. Strike or no strike, the *Titanic* needed nearly 5,000 tons of coal to make it to New York City. Fortunately, Harland and Wolff was able to get coal from their other ships, averting disaster and keeping the journey on schedule.

Food also had to be purchased—enough to feed 2,233 people for a voyage of nearly six days. The refrigerated cargo hold—which included 36,000 apples and 36,000 oranges!—would be stuffed to the gills by the time the *Titanic* set sail.

After loading the ship with supplies, crew members, and the first round of passengers in Southampton, the *Titanic* made stops in Cherbourg, France, and Queenstown, Ireland, to pick up more passengers.

Then, at 1:30 p.m. on April 11, with 333 first-class passengers, 282 second-class passengers, 710 third-class passengers, and 908 crew members on board, the ship set out for New York City.

Thousands of people gathered to wish the *Titanic* a safe maiden voyage.

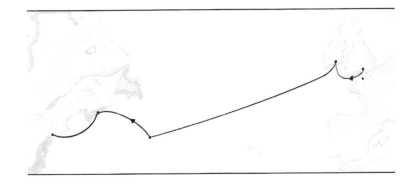

The *Titanic* picked up passengers in Southampton, England; Cherbourg, France; and Queenstown, Ireland. It was meant to steam on to New York City but vanished in the Atlantic.

Aboard the Titanic

What was it like for a passenger on the *Titanic*? The answer depends on how much money they spent to book passage.

THIRD-CLASS LIFE

Passengers in third class, also known as **steerage**, paid between $15 and $40 per person for their place in a cabin. That would be between $402 and $1,073 today. There were a few third-class family cabins, but most people shared small rooms with between two and six wall-mounted single beds.

Most third-class cabins were near the boiler rooms. They were small and noisy but clean and comfortable.

All of the third-class passengers had only two bathtubs to share, but most passengers cleaned up with the soap and water basins included in every *Titanic* stateroom.

There were plenty of toilets on the *Titanic*, though—285, along with 41 urinals.

Three meals a day were included for the price of a ticket. They were all served in the dining room on the F Deck. Only 473 people could be seated in the third-class dining room at a time. So all meals were served twice to feed all 710 steerage passengers. The meals were huge—and better than most people typically enjoyed at home.

Here's a sample menu for a single day:

Breakfast: oatmeal, vegetable stew, fried **tripe** with onions, bread and butter, marmalade, milk, tea and coffee.

Lunch: roast beef and brown gravy, green beans, potatoes, biscuits, prunes, milk, coffee and tea.

Dinner: rabbit pie, baked potatoes, bread and butter, ginger jam, milk, coffee and tea.

If third-class passengers missed a meal, they went hungry until the next scheduled service, since there were no third-class restaurants.

When they weren't eating or sleeping, third-class passengers could enjoy recreational activities in the

General Room on the C Deck. It was filled with beautiful polished wooden benches and card tables. But it was the piano that really raised their spirits and could be played with flair. And when musical passengers brought instruments of their own, it was hard not to dance and sing along. Passengers could also go to the smoking room for ale and cigars. Each class had its own smoking room.

Third class was simple, compared with second and first class. But it was far nicer than any third-class lodging offered by White Star's competition. White Star wanted to make their steerage customers feel welcome. Most third-class passengers hoped their new lives in America would become as grand as their time on the *Titanic* was . . . at first.

SECOND-CLASS EXPERIENCE

Second-class passengers paid about $60 per person ($1,609 today) for a place on the *Titanic*. Most of their cabins were in the **aft,** or back, of the **midship**, between the D and F Decks. They were smaller but almost as lovely as the first-class quarters.

The oak paneling in the second-class staterooms was painted white. The furniture was made of mahogany and included a bed or beds, a large sofa, a wardrobe cabinet, a dressing table with a washbasin, a mirror, and storage shelving.

As in third class, all ticket holders in second class were guaranteed three square meals a day in their exclusive dining room on the D Deck. Second-class chairs were bolted to the dining room floors in case the seas got rough. Second-class meals were even bigger than third-class meals. Here's a partial sample:

Breakfast: fruit, fish, ox kidneys, bacon, sausage, potatoes, ham, eggs, scones, pancakes, syrup, marmalade, coffee and tea.

Lunch: soup, spaghetti, corned beef, dumplings, lamb, roast beef, sausage, ox tongue, pickles, salad, pudding, apple tarts, fresh fruit, cheese, biscuits, coffee and tea.

Dinner in three courses: first course—soup, tapioca; second course—fish, chicken, rice, lamb, turkey, cranberry sauce, peas, turnips, potatoes; third course—pudding, jelly, ice cream, nuts, fresh fruit, cheese, coffee and tea.

Second class also had a library. Filled with bookshelves, writing tables, and comfortable chairs, it was a place to meet quietly with friends for tea or coffee.

Add a barbershop, a beautiful wooden staircase, an electric elevator, and three walking decks called promenades, and you have a clear sense of second-class life. They could even rent deck chairs for $1 to watch the Atlantic Ocean roll by.

Like those in third class, second-class passengers had to share bathtubs, but they had more than two. With a word to the bath **steward**, the lukewarm luxury was within reach.

> *When anyone asks how I can best describe my experience in nearly forty years at sea, I merely say, uneventful. Of course there have been winter gales, and storms and fog and the like, but in all my experience, I have never been in any accident of any sort worth speaking about. I never saw a wreck and never have been wrecked, nor was I ever in any predicament that threatened to end in disaster of any sort.*
>
> —E. J. Smith, captain of the *Titanic*

Parlor staterooms were expensive but luxurious.

FIRST-CLASS LUXURY

As good as second class was, first class was far more luxurious. The *Titanic* was nicknamed "the Millionaire's Special" for a reason. Tickets for first-class staterooms on the B and C Decks started at $150 for smaller cabins, but the price soared to $4,350 for a spacious two-parlor suite with a private outdoor deck. That would be $4,024 to $116,700 today. Only a few suites on the B Deck had private bathrooms with soaking tubs. Those very costly staterooms went to people dripping with money.

FUN FACT: CAPTAIN SMITH'S LAST VOYAGE

Captain Edward J. Smith was born in England on January 27, 1850. He dropped out of school as a 12-year-old and went to sea as a teen. He joined the White Star ranks in 1880, when he was 30. For more than 30 years, he served the company very well and was known as the "Millionaire's Captain" due to his popularity with wealthy passengers. His voyage on the *Titanic* was meant to be a celebration—one last trip before he retired.

PARADE OF RICHES

First-class passengers enjoyed linen tablecloths and napkins. Their meals were served on fine china that boasted the White Star Line's logo. Dinner was the most formal meal.

Each night, wealthy men dressed in tuxedos. Women wore their finest gowns, furs, and jewelry. As they gathered for their nightly 10-course dinners, they walked down one of the ship's most impressive features—the Grand Staircase—or took the electric elevators reserved just for them.

From the *Titanic*'s first-class quarters, the 60-foot Grand Staircase bridged six different decks. Built of polished oak, it began as two staircases on either side that met in the middle on a large landing.

The Grand Staircase was rebuilt for the 1997 James Cameron film *Titanic*.

On the back wall of the landing, two large angels carved of the finest mahogany seemed to embrace either side of a massive clock. French-style black wrought iron curled like ivy between the staircase banisters and the top of each step.

At the foot of the Grand Staircase, a bronze statue of a **cherub** was mounted. The baby-angel features of cherubs were often seen in French and British **classical** paintings. This cherub held a torch-shaped lamp that shined like an electric flame. Only the glass dome above the staircase glowed brighter.

What did first-class passengers eat? A lot! This is just a partial list:

Breakfast: baked apples, fresh fruit, oatmeal, rice, salmon, lamb, bacon, ham, sausage, eggs (fried, poached, boiled, or omelet), steak, potatoes, rolls, scones, corn bread, pancakes, honey, marmalade, coffee, tea, and milk.

Lunch: broth, soup, fish, eggs, chicken, corned beef, vegetables, dumplings, lamb, potatoes (mashed, fried, or baked), pudding, pasties, salmon, shrimp, sardines, roast beef, bologna, ox tongue, lettuce, tomatoes, and eight kinds of cheese.

Dinner: oysters, soup, salmon, cucumbers, filet mignon, chicken, lamb, roast duckling, applesauce, sirloin of beef, potatoes, peas, carrots, rice, lettuce, squab, asparagus, celery, pudding, peaches, chocolate or vanilla eclairs, and ice cream.

If nothing on the menu looked appetizing, first-class passengers could pay extra to eat at three expensive *Titanic* restaurants—the À la Carte, the Café Parisien, and the Verandah Café, also called the Palm Court—side by side on the B Deck bridge.

Before or after dinner, first-class passengers could make use of the gymnasium to exercise—complete with an electric bull and an electric camel. They could relax in the *Titanic*'s Turkish bath, where they would be massaged with fine oils and bathed by hand. Or they could swim in the ship's indoor saltwater pool.

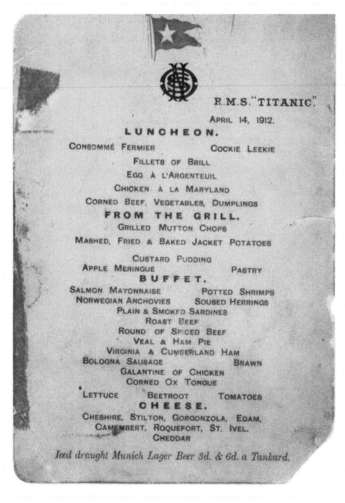

Even lunch was a feast on the *Titanic*.

Regardless of class, every *Titanic* passenger was about to have an experience they would not soon forget aboard the infamous "ship of dreams."

FUN FACT: STROLLING THE PROMENADE

White Star went to great lengths to please first-class travelers, especially when it came to the first-class promenade on the A Deck. The luxurious 200-foot, open-air space was partially enclosed to provide the wealthy a place to walk

without fear of the weather. If passengers wanted to rest, they could lounge in deck chairs. They could also ask the steward for games to play, including shuffleboard, dominoes, and chess. The promenade was accessible from the beautiful Grand Staircase, the Verandah Café/Palm Court restaurant, and the aft staircase. Even the Boat Deck was open to first-class passengers, with all lifeboats pushed far to either side to provide better views and more room to wander.

The First Three Days

For the first three days, everything ran smoothly on the *Titanic*. Captain Smith ordered "full steam ahead," meaning he wanted to run the ship at maximum speed as she cut through the Atlantic Ocean. As expected, the *Titanic* made excellent time at 21 knots.

April 11, day one: she sailed 484 miles

April 12, day two: she sailed 519 miles

April 13, day three: she sailed 546 miles

As April 13 ended, the *Titanic* had sailed 1,549 miles, just under half of the 3,419-mile distance between Southampton and New York. But as she pressed on, the fate of the ship took a dangerous turn when the ocean currents picked up speed.

CHAPTER 3

The Iceberg

Wireless Warnings

The *Titanic* had the best wireless communications equipment money could buy. With the **electro-magnetic** radios in place, messages could be sent by **Morse code** to other radios within a 500-mile **radius.**

Housed in the tiny Marconi Room, a space named for the equipment's inventor, Guglielmo Marconi, the radio was manned by two expert operators, Jack Phillips, age 25, and Harold Bride, age 22. White Star considered the radio room more a luxury service for the passengers than a safety measure.

For the first three days, Phillips and Bride stayed busy sending personal messages from wealthy passengers to their contacts on dry land—each for a handsome fee. When Phillips slept, Bride manned the radio. When Bride slept, Phillips took over.

Ice warnings from other ships started to arrive on April 11. By April 14, the pace of the warnings had picked up:

→ At 9:00 a.m., a message from the eastbound *Caronia* said, "Captain, *Titanic*—West-bound steamers report **bergs, growlers**, and field ice. . . ." It was delivered to Captain Smith, who shared it with the other officers on the bridge.

→ At 1:42 p.m., the eastbound *Baltic II* warned, "Greek steamer *Athenia* reports passing icebergs and large quantities of field ice. . . ." It was delivered to Captain Smith, who handed it to Bruce Ismay. Ismay showed it to passengers before the captain retrieved it and posted it on the bridge.

→ At 5:50 p.m., Captain Smith altered the course of the *Titanic* slightly in response to the ice warnings, but he did not slow her speed.

→ At 6:30 p.m., the *Californian* sent a message to the *Antillian*. The *Titanic*'s radio operators overheard that warning, too. "Three large bergs 5 miles to the south of us." The message was delivered to the bridge, but Captain Smith never saw it. He was dining with first-class passengers at the time.

→ At 9:40 p.m., the *Mesaba* sent another warning. "From *Mesaba* to *Titanic*. Saw much heavy pack ice and great number of large icebergs, also field ice, weather good, clear." The message never made it to the bridge. The radio operator was too busy sending passenger messages to deliver it. So the *Titanic* motored on.

At 10:55 p.m., the nearby *Californian* sent a final warning: "Say, old man. We are stopped and surrounded by ice." Phillips, swamped with passenger messages, replied, "Shut up! Shut up! I am busy." The *Californian* shut its wireless system down for the night, as it did every night it was at sea. It did not receive the *Titanic*'s panicked cries for help until morning, when it was far too late to lend assistance.

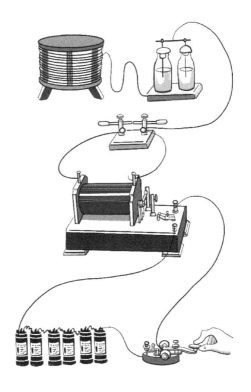

Radio operators used electrical sparks and Morse code to send wireless messages from this device.

DEEP DIVE: HOW WIRELESS WORKED

Marconi's radiotelegraph was the best marine communication device available in 1912, but it was nothing like what we use today. The operators used a key to type the letters of the alphabet in Morse code—a series of dots and dashes for each letter in each word. From the key, a spark or electrical current traveled through a series of tubes and wires mounted in the *Titanic*'s radio room, just one level down from the upper boat deck. The currents then traveled to a wireless antenna mounted on the boat deck, where they were sent as electrical waves to any receivers close enough to capture them. It was impossible to send a message to one receiver—privately. Anyone with a wireless system could read them, as long as they knew Morse code.

RIGHT AHEAD!

About an hour before the *Californian*'s final message of the night, lookout men Frederick Fleet and Reginald Lee climbed 50 feet to the **crow's nest** for their two-hour watch duties. They had no binoculars. The key to the binocular locker was still in merchant seaman David Blair's pocket. Blair had originally been part of the crew, but he was removed from his post when the crew was reorganized shortly before the

Titanic departed. Fleet and Lee had to manage without the binoculars.

They knew nothing of the radio room's iceberg warnings. They only knew the night was bitter cold, the ocean was calm, and the sky was filled with too many stars to count. All was well until Fleet saw a shadow approaching 20 minutes before his shift was set to end.

When he realized what had created the shadow, he rang the bell three times, a signal of approaching danger. And his fateful cry rang out: "Iceberg," he shouted into the crow's nest telephone at the top of his lungs, "right ahead!"

First Officer William Murdoch sounded the order: turn the *Titanic* "hard a-starboard," or quickly to the left, and reverse engines. But it was too late.

At 11:40 p.m., as the jagged ice hit the hull just past the bow, it screamed and scraped, popping rivets and opening up the *Titanic*'s side. Alarmed by the impact, Captain Smith rushed to the bridge to investigate. He was told the mailroom had been flooded with icy seawater. Soon after, at least five of the engine room compartments were also flooded, though the emergency watertight doors had shut automatically, as planned.

Striking the iceberg sealed the *Titanic*'s fate.

Ship's designer Thomas Andrews soon confirmed the captain's worst fears. There would be no saving their "unsinkable" ship, but they could try to save some of her passengers. They would have to act quickly, though, because Andrews believed the *Titanic* would be on the floor of the North Atlantic in two hours or less.

The *Titanic* was just 400 miles south of Newfoundland, Canada—another day's cruise away. It was only 1,246 miles from New York.

MAN THE LIFEBOATS

By midnight, the crew was preparing to load passengers into lifeboats. Seven were stored on each side of the *Titanic*'s boat deck—two groups of three at the forward end, and two groups of four at the back end.

Two others, called cutters, which were normally used to rescue people who had fallen overboard, were on the back side of the bridge, one to the right, one to the left.

Two more collapsible lifeboats were stored under the cutters and two more on top of the officers' quarters, which were also on the boat deck.

There was space for only 1,178 people

The *Titanic*'s crew tried to save as many passengers as possible, with women and children loaded onto lifeboats first.

on all 20 lifeboats. But there were 2,233 on board the ship. So, the impossible order was given: women and children first.

SOS—SAVE OUR SOULS

As the *Titanic*'s crew went door-to-door warning passengers and handing out life jackets, Phillips and Bride radioed for help. It was now April 15, 1912.

- **12:15 a.m.** – *Titanic* to any ship: "CQD." "CQ" was a general call signal used that was derived from the sound of the pronunciation of the French *sécu*, part of the French word *sécurité* (meaning "safety"). "D," which stands for "distress," was added to signal a distress call.
- **12:17 a.m.** – *Titanic* to any ship: "CQD, CQD, SOS. Require immediate assistance. Come at once. We struck an iceberg. Sinking." Two ships responded, the *Frankfurt*, 170 miles away, and the *Olympic*, 500 miles away.
- **12:20 a.m.** – *Titanic* to *Carpathia*: "Come at once. We have struck a berg. It's a CQD, old man."
- **12:21 a.m.** – *Carpathia* to *Titanic*: "I say, old man, do you know there is a batch of messages coming through for you from MCC/Cape Cod?"
- **12:22 a.m.** – *Titanic* to *Carpathia*: "CQD CQD."
- **12:25 a.m.** – *Carpathia* to *Titanic*: "Shall I tell my captain? Do you require assistance?"
- **12:26 a.m.** – *Titanic* to *Carpathia*: "Yes, come quick!"
- **12:32 a.m.** – *Carpathia* to *Titanic*: "Putting about and heading for you." She was 58 miles away.
- **12:40 a.m.** – *Titanic* to *Carpathia*: "SOS *Titanic* sinking by the head. We are about all down. Sinking . . ."

With the *Carpathia* on the way, the *Titanic* continued to radio for help until they lost all power at about 2:25 a.m. They hoped a closer ship might respond. Nine ships received the calls, and several promised help, but the *Carpathia* was the first to make good on that promise.

The ship closest to the *Titanic* was the *Californian*, locked in ice just 20 miles away as night fell. But its wireless operator didn't get the messages until morning—far too late to offer any help.

Many ships at sea heard *Titanic*'s wireless cries for help before she sank.

Lifeboat 7 was the first to load. Though it was meant to hold 65 people, it was lowered at 12:45 a.m. with just 28 people on board.

Lifeboat 5 quietly left just ten minutes later. When Lifeboat 4 left the ship around 1:55 a.m., John J. Astor, the richest man on the *Titanic*, refused to board. "We are safer on board the ship than in this little boat," he said. Astor was wrong, but many passengers agreed with him. Most lifeboats left with multiple seats empty. By the time all 16 traditional lifeboats were gone, far more people were left on the ship than had escaped.

> *If they are sending the boats away, they might as well put some people in them.*
>
> —Walter Hurst, *Titanic* greaser

Collapsible Lifeboats A, B, C, and D—each with seats for 47 people—were all that remained. Only 188 more people had even a prayer of surviving the *Titanic*. Collapsible Lifeboat C carried 44 people, but Collapsible Lifeboat D left with only 25 on board. A few more people leapt into the sea and swam to the safety of Collapsible Lifeboat C after it was set adrift.

As Collapsible Lifeboats A and B were retrieved from storage at 2:12 a.m., the *Titanic* was about to split in two.

Frigid salt water rushed across the boat deck, sending Lifeboats A and B tumbling into the sea. Wireless operator Harold Bride was washed into the ocean along with them.

With every lifeboat gone, the remaining passengers and crew had only two choices. They could go down with the ship, or they could chance jumping into the ocean and treading water. With the water temperature at just 28 degrees Fahrenheit, most who took that leap died within 10 minutes, due to **hypothermia.** Even so, hundreds were willing to take that chance.

> *Striking the water was like a thousand knives being driven into one's body.*
> —Charles Lightoller, second officer of the *Titanic*

Many without seats on lifeboats took their chances in the icy sea.

Some survived the chill, including Harold Bride, who emerged from beneath Collapsible Lifeboat B. An air pocket had saved his life.

Swimmers who tried to make their way to Collapsible Lifeboat A were not as lucky. Most slipped, lifeless, into the dark water before reaching the boat. In the end, fate delivered only 705 traumatized people to safety. Those who lived were forced to witness the deaths of 1,503 fellow passengers—to listen to their dying screams, followed by the deafening silence of their deaths.

In that heartbreaking, frozen silence, they could only wait and pray that a second ship would arrive to save them—again.

> *The sound of people drowning is something that I cannot describe to you, and neither can anyone else. It's the most dreadful sound and there is a terrible silence that follows it.*
>
> —Eva Hart, seven-year-old *Titanic* passenger

MESSAGE IN A BOTTLE

Jeremiah Burke was only 19 when he boarded the *Titanic* as a third-class passenger from Glanmire, County Cork, Ireland. His sisters had already emigrated to America and he wanted to follow them.

When the ship hit the iceberg, Jeremiah grabbed a slip of paper and wrote a simple note.

FROM TITANIC, GOODBYE ALL. BURKE OF GLANMIRE, CORK.

He rolled the paper up and reached for the bottle of holy water his mother had given him. Faith for his journey, she must have thought. He used every ounce of that faith to empty the bottle, slide the note inside, wrap his shoelace around the neck of the bottle, and throw it overboard.

One year after he drowned, the bottle washed up on the shores of Ireland, only a few miles from his family's farm. His mother recognized his handwriting.

His family kept the precious note until 2011, when they donated it to the Cobh Heritage Centre—a tribute to Jeremiah and all the loved ones of Cork lost on the ship of dreams.

Why did the people in the lifeboats let so many of their shipmates freeze to death in the North Atlantic? Why didn't they row back to save a few more souls?

Some were afraid that as the *Titanic* sank, it would suck the lifeboats down with it. The only safe choice was to row as far as you could from the ship, as fast as you could.

Others feared the panicked people in the water would sink the lifeboats trying to save them. But the boats were especially made not to sink, so that was unlikely.

A few may have been too selfish, thinking that if they were safe, what did the others matter?

We may never know which passengers fell into each of those three categories. And we may never know countless reasons of their own. We only know that more people could have survived the disaster had their choices been different.

CAREER INSIDER: MARINE ENGINEER

Chief Engineering Officer Joseph Bell commanded a staff of 24 engineers, 6 electrical engineers, 2 boilermakers, a plumber, and a clerk on the *Titanic*. As educated professionals, they were paid more than most crew members, but their responsibilities were greater, too. From engines, to boilers, to furnaces, to electric generators, to general plumbing, these men were in charge of every mechanical function on the ship.

As the *Titanic* took on water, it was Bell's team that fought for time to save as many passengers as possible. They pumped out water, managed the steam in the engines, and kept the generators working to maintain the ship's lights. When the battle was lost, all 34 men, including Bell, went down with the ship.

Today's marine engineers follow in their proud footsteps. On modern ships, they maintain the same mechanical functions Bell's staff managed, plus **sonar**, fuel oil **bunkering**, electrical fuel cells (big batteries), air-conditioning, laying oceanic cable, maintaining underwater vehicles and cameras, and keeping detailed records.

Accidents like those that destroyed the *Titanic* are far less likely in the modern age. And it is the engineering profession that has helped make this possible. When the *Titanic* Engineers' Memorial opened in Southampton on April 22, 1914, two years and one week after the brave crewmen of the *Titanic* perished, it became a tribute to all marine engineers who courageously carry out their duties—past, present, and future.

THE BREAKUP

The mighty *Titanic*, once ablaze with electric lights, slowly blacked out. Hundreds of people were still on board, including the cooks, doctors, engineers, stewards, and officers who held their duty to their passengers above their duty to themselves. Those faithful people were now struggling to survive in the dark.

Hopelessness must have spread when the once-unsinkable ship grumbled and growled and started to split in half. It began with two heavy pieces of the ship's double-bottom construction. Their rivets failed and they tumbled to the bottom of the sea first.

The bow, flooded with seawater and growing heavier by the minute, was pulled by the forces of gravity to follow the broken pieces. When it finally broke away from the stern, it fell 12,500 feet to the bottom of the sea—like a stone. The heavy boilers crashed through the ship as it tore.

Released from the weight of the bow, the back of the ship rose in the air, practically standing on end in the water, before it followed the rest of the ship to the ocean floor. After a fierce battle two hours and forty minutes long, the *Titanic* simply vanished.

ome people did not believe witnesses who said the *Titanic* broke in half, but they re correct.

FUN FACT: ONE PIECE OR TWO?

When investigators interviewed the surviving passengers of the *Titanic*, not all of their stories matched. Most said the ship sank in one piece, right before their eyes. But 15 people insisted it broke in half before it disappeared.

"She snapped in two, and the bow went down and the aft part came up and stayed up five minutes before it went down," said one *Titanic* seaman during a United States senatorial investigation in 1912. "We were quite near her and could see her quite plainly," he continued.

Nonsense, said experts. "It was believed the survivors were under a lot of stress and weren't in command of their faculties," was how New York City College technology professor Rich Woytowich put it. "Their testimony just wasn't **credible**."

Turns out the experts were wrong. In 2012, Professor Woytowich and other engineers concluded that the ship did snap in two. The 15 eagle-eyed passenger witnesses were long gone, but the truth restored their reputations.

To the Rescue

First launched in 1902, the *Carpathia* was built to carry immigrants to and from America, running at

14 steady knots as she went. She never tried to dazzle millionaires. And yet, it was the *Carpathia* that came to luxury's rescue.

Survivors in one of the collapsible lifeboats were relieved to see the *Carpathia* arrive just after dawn.

Arthur Rostron, age 42, was captain of the *Carpathia*. His wireless operator, Harold Cottam, received the cry for help at 12:15 a.m. on April 15, just as he bent down to untie his shoes and prepare for bed. Immediately, Cottam shared the message with Captain Rostron. After a few moments of horrified disbelief, Rostron and the *Carpathia* changed course.

The ship was 58 miles from the *Titanic*'s last reported location. At 14 knots, it would take three and a half hours to reach the stranded survivors.

Rooms were emptied, the doctors were alerted, blankets and warm clothes were collected. Servings of hot tea, coffee, and soup were ready even before the *Carpathia* reached her destination.

After dodging a sea of dangerous icebergs like the one that had disabled the *Titanic*, and pushing its engines to near 17 knots, the *Carpathia* was just north of the *Titanic*'s last radioed position. A bright green flare rose from one of the waiting lifeboats. The first survivors were on board the *Carpathia* by 4:10 a.m. and the last by 8:30 a.m.

Mrs. Charlotte Collyer and her daughter Marjorie both survived the sinking of the *Titanic*.

The *Carpathia* slowly moved through the field of wreckage, searching for more survivors, but found no one alive. It soon headed for New York.

When she arrived at Pier 54 on the evening of April 18, the *Carpathia* found reporters gathered to greet it, screaming questions through **megaphones**. But that wasn't Captain Rostron's proudest moment. Helping

The *Carpathia* carried the survivors to safety in New York City.

save 705 souls was what made him proud. "A hand other than mine was on the wheel that night," he said.

The *Carpathia* collected the living survivors of the *Titanic* disaster. But the gruesome task of bringing home the lifeless fell to four other ships—the CS *Mackay-Bennett*, the CS *Minia*, the CGS *Montmagny*, and the SS *Algerine*. They returned between 316 and 337 bodies to their loved ones. Roughly 1,160 bodies were never found.

> *With the exception of about 10 bodies that had received serious injuries, their looks were calm and peaceful.*
> —Dr. Thomas Armstrong, ship's surgeon of the *Mackay-Bennett*

THE MYSTERY OF THE TITANIC

For decades, the *Titanic* was missing in action. But when the US Navy decided to search for two sunken nuclear submarines in the 1980s, the tragedies **intersected**.

The USS *Thresher* sank on April 10, 1963, and The USS *Scorpion* was lost on May 22, 1968. Both sank with the nuclear reactors that powered them, but the *Scorpion* also had nuclear weapons. The navy wanted to collect information without the Russian military's knowing.

In 1982, **oceanographer** Dr. Robert Ballard asked the navy for money to pursue his dream of finding the *Titanic*. Deputy Chief of Naval Operations Ronald Thunman said yes, on one condition: Ballard had to find and explore the two lost submarines first.

If it took too long to find and evaluate the *Thresher* and the *Scorpion*, there would be no time or money left to search for the *Titanic*. But Ballard agreed.

CHAPTER 4

Testing the Tech

Ballard had searched for the *Titanic*—unsuccessfully—once before. In October 1977, he had teamed up with the Alcoa Corporation—one of the world's biggest producers of **aluminum** products—to find the sunken ship. On their **salvage** ship the *Seaprobe*, Ballard and Alcoa had hoped to use sonar and cameras attached to the ship's deep-sea drilling arm to find and identify the wreck. They had also hoped to lift parts of the *Titanic* to the surface by remote control.

That effort ended with $600,000 worth of equipment crashing to the bottom of the North Atlantic and nothing to show for it. That would be over $2.5 million today.

But Ballard had an excellent reputation; he had served in the Navy Reserve at the Woods Hole Oceanographic Institution (WHOI) in Massachusetts for many years. One of his career highlights was helping them bring the *Alvin* to life in the early 1970s.

The *Alvin* was a small submarine called a **submersible** that could carry a pilot and two scientists 14,800 feet down to the ocean floor to do research. Thanks to the

Alvin and other submersibles, Ballard had been able to explore both the Mid-Atlantic Ridge and deepwater **hydrothermal vents** in the Galápagos Rift. The US Navy took notice of this work, though Ballard still thought he could do better.

Moving between the ocean's surface and ocean floor took two and a half hours in the *Alvin*, a commute of five hours each day. That left only three hours a day to gather information. The cramped quarters and deep-water pressures were hard on the human body.

Eager for more time to safely see and explore the depths, Ballard came up with a new idea he called "telepresence." His team explored the possibility of using

Underwater robots captured pictures of the *Titanic* shipwreck.

remote-controlled mini-robots with lights and cameras attached. By the time Ballard approached the navy about funding, WHOI had created Argo, an undersea video sled with lights and cameras they could send to the ocean floor. They nicknamed the first robotic camera "Jason Jr." ("JJ" for short) after the mythological Greek hero who led the **Argonauts**.

JJ could move by remote control to locations up to 20,000 feet in depth, and the scientists could control the lights and JJ from the ship above. JJ could transmit video images electronically to the surface, where men at computers could catalog and analyze them.

Ballard was hoping to test the new technology on the *Titanic*. The navy knew it could help with their submarines, too, but they feared the search for the *Titanic* would draw too much attention to their secret mission.

Turns out, the *Titanic* was a great cover story. All three wrecks were in the northern Atlantic Ocean. If the Russians thought the navy and their partners at the French Research Institute for Exploitation of the Sea were only looking for the *Titanic*, the nuclear submarines would never cross their minds.

FUN FACT: THE TITANIC'S TEXAN (AND HIS PET MONKEY)

Schemes to find the *Titanic* were not unusual after the luxury ship disappeared. But Texas oil millionaire Jack Grimm was one of the most determined of hunters.

By the time he turned his sights on the *Titanic*, he had already financed searches for Bigfoot, the Loch Ness Monster, and Noah's Ark.

In 1980, he boarded the research ship HJW *Fay* with support from Columbia University and scientists from the Scripps Institution of Oceanography. He nearly lost his scientists when he claimed his pet monkey, Titan, would reveal the *Titanic*'s true location by pointing to a place on a map. They stayed, but the mission failed, even with Grimm's magic monkey.

In 1981, the millionaire and his team tried again on the research ship the *Gyre*, but the weather made any serious search impossible. Grimm insisted the ship's sonar spotted one of the *Titanic*'s anchors or a propeller, but his experts refused to support the claim.

Grimm's last attempt came in 1983 aboard a ship called the *Robert D. Conrad*. Once again, bad weather foiled the scheme. But when his course was later reviewed, it was proven he had passed directly over the *Titanic*— without knowing it.

It was a great deal for the navy, but Ballard knew there were no guarantees. Officially, he had 60 days to find and study two submarines. Would there be enough time left for the *Titanic* once that mission was accomplished?

With a team from the navy and WHOI aboard the naval research ship the *Knorr*, Ballard began to investigate the subs. As he worked, Ballard observed that the wreckage of the *Scorpion* and the *Thresher* had fallen in pieces along the seabed. The heaviest parts had fallen first, whereas the lighter bits had settled more slowly, carried by northern ocean currents.

"I was thinking it was going to be a circular pile of stuff, and it was a comet instead," he said. This information helped crack the *Titanic* code.

Ballard completed his naval assignment with just 12 days left to use the *Knorr*'s equipment, including JJ and Argo, to search for the *Titanic*. But he had help from the French.

The search for the *Titanic*—code-named "White Star"—began on board the French ship *Le Suroît* on June 28, 1985. A crew of 47 people, including experts from the navy, WHOI, and the French Research Institute for Exploitation of the Sea, set out to succeed where so many others had failed.

FUN FACT: WILL THIS WORK? NOPE!

Almost as soon as the *Titanic* vanished into the North Atlantic, people began to suggest crazy schemes to raise her back to the surface—assuming she was ever found. They include:

1. **Filling her with Ping-Pong balls.** Although Ping-Pong balls do float, they could never survive the pressure of *Titanic*'s two-and-a-half-mile ocean depths.

2. **Filling her with petroleum jelly.** Inserting thousands of watertight bags of petroleum jelly into the wreckage would likely add bulk, not lift it up.

3. **Freezing her.** Engineers suggested wrapping the wreck in a wire-mesh frame, then pumping it full of **liquid nitrogen**. But a wire frame could not contain the liquid nitrogen.

4. **Pumping her full of hot wax.** Wax does float as it cools to a solid, but keeping millions of gallons hot enough to fill the wreck of the *Titanic* would be impossible.

5. **Blowing her up.** Five days after the *Titanic* went down, Vincent Astor, whose millionaire father John J. Astor went down with the ship, wanted to blow the wreckage to bits to free the trapped victims' bodies. He didn't consider the fact that the bodies would explode with the ship.

CHAPTER 5

Finding the Titanic

A French/American Partnership

Oceanographer Dr. Robert Ballard dreamed of finding the lost *Titanic*.

Although Dr. Robert Ballard is the face of the *Titanic*'s rediscovery, it was a French/American partnership that actually made the find possible. Ballard's French counterpart was Dr. Jean-Louis Michel of the French Research Institute for Exploitation of the Sea (IFREMER), which did much of the mission's prep work.

Ballard was searching for the navy's lost submarines, so the French started conducting studies without him. *Le Suroît* left port on July 1, 1985, with the finest sonar technology available. They would conduct the most careful search for the *Titanic* ever attempted.

Using logbooks from ships sailing near the *Titanic* when she sank, eyewitness testimonies, distress calls sent by the *Titanic*'s wireless operators, and weather and current reports from previous search teams, they narrowed the search area to 100 square miles.

Michel joined Ballard on the *Knorr* when the ship arrived to pick up where the French had left off. But instead of looking for large chunks of wreckage, they looked for small debris. Ballard's search for the *Scorpion* and the *Thresher* had taught him wreckage in the North Atlantic could be spread out over a long stretch of the seafloor.

Ballard compared the small debris pieces to footprints in the snow that would lead to the bigger discoveries, and he was right. But he didn't know it right away. At first, the scraps on sonar were "just stuff," he said. But when Michel spotted what looked like metal at 12:43 a.m. on September 1, the "stuff" was suddenly important.

The metal turned out to be one of the *Titanic*'s 29 coal-fired boilers, a 57-ton piece of machinery the size of a two-car garage. The team had hit pay dirt.

A really big target was discovered at roughly 2:00 a.m. The French team had only missed the front of the lost ship by 200 meters—just a little more than one-tenth of a mile. If they had not already searched an area six times the size of Manhattan, Ballard might not have expanded the search zone and the *Titanic* might still be lost. The battered hull of the *Titanic*'s bow was resting in 60 feet of ocean silt a full 13 miles southeast of its expected location, meaning that the rescue coordinates radio operators Jack Phillips and Harold Bride frantically wired in 1912 were wrong. It took both the French and the American explorers to make the discovery happen.

When the *Knorr* launched Argo and JJ, the team could see beyond sonar imaging. They were able to recognize parts of the *Titanic* that had been lost for 73 years. Argo's lights shined as JJ's video cameras picked up the gleaming brass of the **porthole** frames, the unbroken glass in cabin windows, the seams of steel held together by thousands of rivets. JJ even spotted the buckled steel panels and popped rivets that were damaged by the iceberg. It was like seeing a dream come true and a nightmare at the same time.

Unfortunately, Ballard's naval funding and time allowance were exhausted before he could find the ship's stern. He made plans to return the following year. The mystery of the *Titanic*'s exact location was finally solved. But there was much more to discover.

The *Knorr* was well equipped to search for the legendary *Titanic*.

CAREER INSIDER: OCEANOGRAPHER

Dr. Robert Ballard has worn many hats during his professional years: naval officer, marine geologist, even college professor. But it is his work as an oceanographer that has drawn the brightest spotlight.

Not only has he revealed the secrets of the *Titanic*, he's expanded our understanding of the last frontier on Earth—the deep waters of the ocean. More than 98 percent of the sea has not yet been explored. Oceanographers hope to change that.

Do you dream of being an oceanographer? Consider reading books on geology, biology, and chemistry, but work hard on math and English, too. Learn to swim, and volunteer to help any organization dedicated to the study and preservation of ocean habitats.

Once you graduate from high school, work toward a college degree in marine biology, geology, chemistry, or physics. Then plan on an advanced degree in one of four kinds of oceanography:

1. Geological oceanography is the study of the ancient history and rocky structure of the ocean floor.
2. Chemical oceanography explores the chemistry of ocean waters, including how pollution impacts ocean habitats.

3. Physical oceanography seeks to understand waves, tides, currents, and the impact of light and sound on the ocean.

4. Biological oceanography focuses on marine life—how species interact and fight to survive in their ocean environments.

"The deep sea is the largest museum on Earth," according to Dr. Ballard. "It contains more history than all the museums on land combined." If you'd like to help explore that mysterious world, oceanography might be in your future.

CHAPTER 6

Why and How Did the Titanic Sink?

When the *Titanic* sideswiped the iceberg, what really happened? There are many theories—and many pieces of evidence to support each one.

> *Deeply regret to advise you, Titanic sank this morning after collision with iceberg resulting in serious loss of life. Full particulars later.*
>
> —J. Bruce Ismay, head of White Star Line

A Frosty Trick of the Light

The spot in the North Atlantic where the accident happened is where two powerful oceanic forces meet—the Gulf Stream and the Labrador Current.

The Gulf Stream is made up of warm southern waters that flow from Mexico and continue up the eastern coast of the United States and Canada. These tropical waters then cross the North Atlantic toward Iceland and England. A circular pattern of strong winds and currents keeps the warm waters moving. The Gulf Stream helps keep Europe's weather milder than it would be without it.

In 1912, the Gulf Stream was even warmer than usual.

The Labrador Current is icy water—always less than 32 degrees Fahrenheit—that flows south from Greenland. And it carries thousands of icebergs from Greenland with it.

The *Titanic* hit the iceberg and sank just where the exceptionally warm Gulf Stream waters intersected with

Did a thermal inversion cause optical illusions in the North Atlantic that night? The answer may be yes.

the cold Labrador Current. At this spot, something called a thermal inversion was formed. It's a layer of cold air below a layer of warm air, and it can bend the light in a way that plays tricks on your eyes, also called **optical illusions**. Even though the night was clear as a bell, a trick of the light may have hidden the iceberg from the *Titanic*'s lookouts.

The *Californian*, just 20 miles away, warned the *Titanic* of ice in wireless messages, but the optical illusions made it nearly impossible for the ship's lookouts to see it. There was so little contrast between the sea and the night sky that the **horizon** looked far more distant than it was. The shadow of the iceberg faded into that horizon, too.

The same optical illusions made the *Titanic* look like a much smaller ship to the *Californian*, much too small and close to be the sinking luxury liner. The warm and cold layers of air also distorted the Morse code distress calls. The *Californian* had no idea the nearby ship they saw was the *Titanic*—the ship pleading for help.

Even the *Titanic*'s distress rockets were distorted by the bend of the light. They were launched 600 feet into the air, but the *Californian* thought they were much lower—and possibly fireworks. When the "small" ship disappeared, it was because the *Titanic* had been swallowed by the Atlantic. But the *Californian* thought the smaller ship had simply sailed away. Her crew didn't know they were close enough to help until it was too late.

Supermoon Mischief?

According to *National Geographic* and astronomer David Olson, a **supermoon**'s impact on regional tides may have contributed to the *Titanic*'s tragic end.

A supermoon is a full moon that passes especially close to Earth. When it does, the sun, the moon, and Earth are positioned in a straight line, increasing the **gravitational** pull on the oceans. Low tides are lower and high tides are higher because of the powerful magnetism.

On January 4, 1912, a supermoon crossed the sky—three months before the *Titanic* sank. It was the closest moon in 600 years. It may have caused more icebergs to break from the shores of Greenland. And it may have freed old icebergs once trapped in the shallows. With higher waters to float them, they could have drifted into the *Titanic*'s path.

The rise in tide would not have been extreme, but according to Olson, it wouldn't have needed to be. "Suppose you pull a rowboat to a beach at low tide," he said in *National Geographic*. "It doesn't have to be much of a higher tide to refloat the rowboat."

That small rise may have helped send the *Titanic* to her doom.

The Iceberg Supreme

In the days that followed the *Titanic* disaster, many ships reported seeing the monster iceberg that caused her destruction—an iceberg that was likely 50 to 100 feet high and 200 to 400 feet long when the collision happened, according to the United States Coast Guard. It was far bigger than most icebergs common to the North Atlantic.

> *The big icebergs that drift into warmer water melt much more rapidly under water than on the surface, and sometimes a sharp, low reef extending two or three hundred feet beneath the sea is formed.*
>
> —E. J. Smith, captain of the *Titanic*

On the morning of April 15, 1912, travelers on the German ocean liner the *Prinz Adalbert* photographed a huge iceberg with a "red smear" at its waterline. Was the red smear seen by German travelers fresh red paint scraped from the hull of the *Titanic*? Does that lend scientific support to estimates of the size of the iceberg that caused such disaster? It seems likely. But one thing was certain: the red-stained iceberg was identical to the monster described by the *Titanic*'s eyewitnesses. Even the *Carpathia* saw the iceberg on her way to rescue the survivors.

Do these two post-*Titanic* sightings prove the theory of the supermoon's high tides releasing an iceberg supreme into the North Atlantic? Did gravity unleash a gigantic piece of floating ice capable of splitting the side of an unsinkable ship? Perhaps.

By the time the cable ship *Minia* searched the region for bodies and debris, the iceberg was much smaller than the monster photographed by the *Prinz Adalbert*. But the *Minia*'s captain, William de Carteret, assumed it was the same iceberg, and he was probably right.

Once the damage was done, the *Titanic*'s iceberg continued its journey through the Atlantic's waters. It was just days away from the warmth of the Gulf Stream, where it continued to melt until it was gone—quickly reclaimed by the sea, like the *Titanic*.

DEEP DIVE: TIDAL TIDBITS

According to the National Oceanic and Atmospheric Administration, the US scientific agency that studies oceans, high tides and low tides are caused by the moon's gravitational pull on Earth. That tugging is known as the tidal force. Earth's ocean waters rise on the sides of the planet that are closest to and most distant from the moon. They rise their highest during a full moon. That rise is known as high tide.

When a coastline is not in one of the bulge positions, it enters into a low tide. Most coastal locations have two high tides and two low tides each day, though some have only one per day. In either case, it takes 24 hours and 50 minutes to complete the cycle.

Penny-Pinching Rivets

Did Harland and Wolff try to save money when they built the *Titanic*? And did those cost-cutting efforts cause the ship's disastrous accident? That depends on whom you ask.

There was no lack of talent at the shipyard. The company was famous for gathering together the best craftsmen in the business to build their ships, including the *Titanic*. The Irish workforce was top-notch. And they were treated well to keep them loyal to the company.

Some experts question the use of iron and steel rivets to secure the steel pieces of the *Titanic*'s hull. Steel rivets were used on the central hull. Iron rivets were used on the stern and bow, where the ship hit the iceberg. But iron is weaker than steel and less reliable.

Timothy Foecke, a **metallurgist** with the National Institute of Standards and Technologies, has carefully studied 40 rivets recovered from the *Titanic* wreck. Eighteen of the 40 showed signs of impurity—waste called slag mixed with the iron when it was melted and formed into rivets. According to Foecke, that waste weakened the rivets and caused them to pop, where pure iron or steel rivets would have held.

"The damage to the ship . . . spanned six compartments," Foecke said in the *Washington Post*. "If that sixth compartment had not been flooding, the ship could have stayed afloat several hours longer," he continued. That extra time bought by better rivets might have saved lives.

Limited Lifeboats

Ship designer Alexander Carlisle demanded the *Titanic* carry 48 lifeboats on her maiden voyage. His request was far higher than the number required by law—only 16. But Carlisle wanted a seat for every passenger. When his request was denied, he left Harland and Wolff forever.

Was Carlisle right? Most experts agree he was. Though the *Titanic* carried 16 standard lifeboats and 4 collapsibles—4 more than was legally required—the law was outdated. Written in 1896, it was crafted to supply smaller ships. And the *Titanic* was famous for its massive size.

The boats the *Titanic* did carry could have saved 1,178 people, in a perfect-world scenario. But the ship had 2,233 passengers and crew members on board. And the launch of those 20 lifeboats was anything but perfect.

Most of the lifeboats were set adrift with seats empty. The first carried only 12 people. It could have saved 48. Instead of 1,178 people, only 705 were carried to safety. And only two lifeboats turned back to take on more passengers when they realized they had room.

Because there wasn't an adequate number of life-boats, 1,503 people perished in the frigid waters of the North Atlantic.

White Star thought too many lifeboats would clutter the deck of the *Titanic*, would restrict the ocean view of the passengers, and might even make them feel uneasy. According to J. Bruce Ismay, too many lifeboats would make the *Titanic* crossing look dangerous. "I'll not have so many little boats, as you call them, cluttering up my decks and putting fear into my passengers," he said.

The partly filled lifeboat standing by about 100 yards away never came back. Why on Earth they never came back is a mystery. How could any human-being fail to heed those cries?
—Jack B. Thayer, *Titanic* passenger

Human Error

"Human error" is a term for the mistakes people make every day. And many blame the sinking of the *Titanic* on a series of mistakes made by people in control of the ship's many functions.

FIRE?
One mistake was a possible fire in one of the *Titanic*'s three-story-tall coal storage bins, which were called

bunkers. According to Irish journalist Senan Molony, pictures of the *Titanic* before she left port reveal a dark discoloration along a 30-foot stretch of the ship's starboard side—the stretch that came in contact with the iceberg.

Molony believes the mark is proof a coal fire weakened the *Titanic*'s hull and caused the damage that sank the "unsinkable" ship. And in 1912, days after the ship sank, the *New York Tribune* published quotes from an anonymous officer on the ship who shoveled coal from the bins into the *Titanic* boilers.

"The fire must have been raging long before she pulled away from her pier in Southampton," the officer said. "Immediately, we began to work on the fire and it took us until Saturday afternoon to extinguish it."

"In my opinion," he continued, "this fire played no small part in the disaster."

Engineers from Imperial College in London confirm that the dark streak in the photograph could have been caused by a fire in the coal bunker. But it was kept quiet to protect White Star's reputation.

SPEED?

Fire was not the *Titanic*'s only problem. Captain Smith's failure to slow the ship's speed is another reason the damage was worse than it might have been. J. Bruce Ismay wanted the *Titanic* to run at full speed to make the best time possible on her first trip to America. When iceberg warnings came in over the wireless radio, Smith refused to slow her pace. Had the ship been going slower, the efforts to avoid the iceberg might have been more effective.

WARNINGS IGNORED?

Were warnings of icebergs ignored? Not at first. Most of the messages were passed on to Captain Smith. And he made his crew aware and changed course at one point to avoid the ice. But when the passenger messages overwhelmed the wireless operators in the Marconi Room, at least one warning was not given to Captain Smith or officers on the bridge.

BINOCULARS?

Would the disaster have been avoided if the lookouts had carried binoculars into the crow's nest? It's possible. And there were binoculars on board the *Titanic*, safe and secure in a locked cabinet. But second Officer David Blair had forgotten to leave the key when he left the *Titanic* before she set sail.

On some evenings, the binoculars might have been lifesaving. But the strange optical illusions would still have been deceptive, binoculars or no binoculars. So the lookouts in the crow's nest might have been destined to sound the alarm a little too late.

RIGHT-SIDE COLLISION?

The *Titanic* stopped its engines and veered left to avoid hitting the iceberg head-on. It even reversed its engines to try to back away from the jagged ice. But some experts say that sealed her fate.

According to former merchant navy sailor Basildon Blair, not adjusting course would have been better. If the ship had hit the iceberg head-on, "all the force would have been transferred to the back of the ship. It wouldn't have ripped open, but crumpled round, so only two or three compartments would have been breached," he said on *Leading Britain's Conversation*, a radio talk show. "It was built to survive with four compartments breached. I don't believe it would have sunk."

Not scraping the hull against the jagged ice might have kept the *Titanic* afloat long enough for help to arrive and saved everyone on board.

CONCEIT?

Was safety secondary on the *Titanic*? Did the people aboard the ill-fated ship believe the exaggerated press reports that claimed the *Titanic* was unsinkable? And if they did, did that overconfidence cause the accident that took more than 1,500 lives?

Oceanographer Dr. Robert Ballard says the answer is no. "It was the captain who ignored the warnings," he said. Perhaps the captain was partially responsible, but there is plenty of blame to go around.

A perfect storm of smaller mistakes combined took the *Titanic* and more than 1,500 people to a watery grave. But in the end, it was a tragic accident. And it is still remembered more than 100 years later.

Will the *Titanic* live on at the bottom of the North Atlantic? A whole team of experts hope the answer is yes. And if they are successful, the resting place of the ship and her victims will live on in new ways that will be respectful of the people who passed away.

> *If you look in your dictionary you will find "Titans," a race of people vainly striving to overcome the forces of nature. Could anything be more unfortunate than such a name, anything more significant?*
>
> —Arthur Rostron, captain of the *Carpathia*

CHAPTER 7

The Titanic's Erosion, Rescue, and Remembrance

In August 2019, Caladan Oceanic, an undersea **expedition** company, mounted a new, eight-day exploration of the wreck of the *Titanic*. Their aim was to study the ocean's impact on the sunken ship and brainstorm ways to protect it in the future.

Erosion

Mollusks and other sea life had long since consumed most of the ship's wood and fabric elements, such as decking and upholstery. But the 2019 expedition hoped to measure more recent decay.

Through five deepwater dives in their Triton 36000/2 submersible, nicknamed the "Limiting Factor," the team discovered that saltwater **corrosion** and metal-eating **bacteria** were **eroding** the historic ship.

"There are **microbes** on the shipwreck that are eating away the iron of the wreck itself, creating 'rusticle' structures, which is a much weaker form of the metal," said expedition scientist Clare Fitzsimmons in *National Geographic*. Dr. Robert Ballard coined the term "rusticles" to describe the rusty icicles he had seen hanging from the *Titanic*. Fitzsimmons noticed they were so fragile they collapsed into a cloud of reddish ocean dust when disturbed.

"The most shocking area of deterioration was the starboard side of the officers' quarters where the captain's quarters were," said *Titanic* historian Parks Stephenson. He suggested the hull was collapsing, crushing once-preserved staterooms.

Dr. Robert Ballard named the rust-colored formations on the *Titanic* "rusticles," because they looked like rusty icicles.

Salvagers and Treasure Hunters

The damage is obvious, but nature isn't the only threat. In a 2004 dive, explorers found the captain's porcelain soaking tub was remarkably well preserved in his stateroom. But by 2019, it had disappeared. It probably fell into the ship's interior, but it could have been salvaged.

> *In every shipwreck, generally someone died. You don't pick up stuff. You don't pick up belt buckles from the Arizona. You don't go to Gettysburg with a shovel. That's why I left everything alone at the Titanic. It's totally disrespectful to pick up anything.*
>
> —Dr. Robert Ballard, oceanographer

Salvage sounds innocent. And saving pieces of the ship sounds like a good idea. But it's tricky. For example, more than 5,500 **artifacts** were gathered from the *Titanic* by a company called Premier Exhibitions Inc. from 1993 to 2004. But when the company filed for bankruptcy, the artifacts, once displayed in an exhibit, went up for auction.

Although the United Kingdom's National Maritime Museum and the National Museums Northern Ireland raised $19.2 million to save the artifacts from private collectors, they were outbid. A group of investors paid $19.5 million for the artifacts.

They said they would use the artifacts in a way people could see and appreciate. But if they decide to sell the rare material to private collectors, not only will pieces of history disappear, so will the last traces of the *Titanic*'s victims.

Among the collection are:

→ The steel first-class entry door once mounted on the *Titanic*'s hull.
→ The bronze cherub at the bottom of the first-class Grand Staircase (which lost a foot when it was forcefully removed).
→ A once-stylish brown bowler hat with black grosgrain ribbon, which was likely worn by one of the ship's wealthier gentlemen.
→ Ceramic marbles that were once held by one of the 113 children on board the *Titanic*. Only 60 of those children survived.

The "Big Piece," a 17-ton section of the *Titanic*'s starboard hull, was also part of the auctioned collection. Salvaged in 1998, its large portholes once lit passenger cabins. Its smaller portholes filled the bathrooms with light.

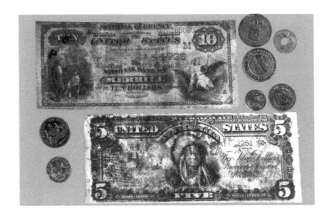

Money recovered from the watery grave of the *Titanic*.

On April 15, 2012, the *Titanic* was added to the United Nations Educational, Scientific and Cultural Organization's Convention on the Protection of the Underwater Cultural Heritage list. The aim was to protect the ship and its artifacts from unauthorized treasure hunters. But the *Titanic* rests in international waters, under no nation's official **jurisdiction.** No one owns the *Titanic*, so it cannot be fully protected.

As a result, many of the *Titanic*'s treasures—many of her secrets—will remain hidden forever.

FUN FACT: BEEP! BEEP!

The 1912 Renault Type CB Coupe de Ville was owned by William Carter, a 36-year-old Pennsylvania coal and iron millionaire. He'd bought the car in Europe and was shipping it home.

Carter and his family found seats on lifeboats, but the car wasn't so lucky. Carter later filed an insurance claim with the White Star Line for $5,000, the 1912 value of the Renault. That's roughly $134,000 today.

Several salvagers have tried to retrieve the car from the wreck of the *Titanic* without success. But they've stopped looking because there is probably little of it left.

A luxury Renault Type CB Coupe de Ville like this one went down with the *Titanic*.

Garbage and Destruction

When underwater explorers retrieve *Titanic* artifacts, they must make room for the added weight on their submersibles. If they pick up a 10-pound treasure, they leave behind 10 pounds of the **ballast** that is used to stabilize the submersible. So, the *Titanic*'s final resting place is now cluttered with abandoned trash.

Even when the submersibles do not stop to gather irreplaceable pieces of history, they can do damage. The *Alvin*, the WHOI's submersible submarine, weighed 17 tons. There is no record of the *Alvin* doing damage, but other submersibles have left a mark. According to Ballard, bright orange patches on the *Titanic*'s deck are evidence of new damage left by careless visitors—and there are far too many visible. Even if the newer submersibles are lighter than the *Alvin*, they still cause damage to the *Titanic*'s fragile surfaces.

Buy a Ticket

Any brave traveler willing to pay $105,129 can hitch a ride on a submersible called the *Titan* to see the *Titanic* for themselves. That's the modern equivalent of a first-class passage on the ship of dreams.

Stockton Rush created OceanGate, the company hosting the expeditions, in 2010 to celebrate the history beneath the ocean's surface.

The *Titan* is made of lighter materials than are used in most submersibles. It carries a pilot, a scientist, and three tourists on every trip. It even has a curtained bathroom.

By combining tourism and science, OceanGate hopes to offer once-in-a-lifetime adventures to the very wealthy, and a means of protecting the *Titanic* through study and observation.

If that price tag is beyond your reach, consider a trip to Ireland. Nestled in the exact spot where Harland and Wolff constructed the *Titanic* is Titanic Belfast, the most complete *Titanic* experience ever created.

For about $25 per person, visitors can explore the Titanic Exhibition Centre, complete with a collection of artifacts, photographs, and newspaper articles. They can join a walking tour of the shipyard, slipways, and Harland and Wolff office buildings. They can watch interactive video programming, have tea near a replica of the Grand Staircase, and so much more.

Until the technology to visit the ship has advanced enough to make our dreams come true, museum exhibits, books, and documentaries will have to quench our thirst for an affordable *Titanic* adventure.

But if we do it right, the dark place where the *Titanic* sank, the place where more than 1,500 people passed away, will remain a scientific wonder and a treasured memorial forever.

GLOSSARY

Wondering what that new word means? Find it here in the glossary, and read the simple definition.

aft: at or near the stern or back of a boat or aircraft

aluminum: a light, silver-gray metal

Argonauts: a group of heroes in Greek mythology

artifact: an object of cultural or historic value

bacteria: tiny, microscopic life-forms that can cause illness or destruction

ballast: something heavy placed on board a ship or other vessel to stabilize it in the water

berg: short for "iceberg"

Board of Trade: a British advisory group that sets rules for trade and shipping

boiler: a container on a ship where coal-heated water is turned into steam to power the steam engines

bow: the front or fore part of a ship or aircraft

bunker: a place to store coal

bunkering: storing fuel oil or coal

catcher: a person who carried red-hot rivets from the fire to the riveters

cherub: an angel in the form of a healthy, plump child with wings

classical: a way to describe ancient music, art, or traditions

corrosion: the slow breakdown of metal or stone

credible: believable, likely to be truthful

crow's nest: a platform at the top of a **mast** used as a lookout station on a ship

cutter: a type of lifeboat usually used to rescue people who fall overboard from a ship

electromagnetic: having to do with the way electricity works with magnetic fields

elegant: graceful and stylish looking

erosion: the process of being slowly carved away by weather, water, or wind

expedition: a journey, sometimes scientific, to discover new facts or places

fitted: finished and made whole with construction and furnishings

fitter: a craftsman who adds cabinetry, plumbing, light fixtures, and other final touches to ships

forward: at the front of the ship

frigid: very cold

funnel: a large smokestack or chimney on a steamship

gantry: a framework structure used in the building of ships

glamour: something that makes a person or place seem exciting and attractive

gravitational: involving the force of gravity in action

greaser: a person who keeps the mechanical parts of a ship greased and running without friction

growler: a small iceberg less than seven feet across with less than four feet showing above the water

horizon: a line in the distance that appears to be where the sky meets the Earth

hull: the outer body of a ship

hydrothermal vent: a structure on the seafloor that releases hot, volcanic water into the ocean

hypothermia: an extremely low body temperature

intersect: cross paths

jurisdiction: the area in which a person or people have the power to make legal decisions

keel: a structure that runs lengthwise along the bottom of a ship, on which the rest of the hull is built

knot: a unit of speed for ships, aircraft, and winds equal to one nautical mile per hour

liquid nitrogen: a thin, colorless liquid used for cooling or freezing things

luxurious: extremely beautiful, comfortable, and expensive

mast: a tall post on a ship or boat

megaphone: a device used to make voices louder

metallurgist: a scientist who works with metal and melted metal mixtures called alloys

microbe: a microscopic life-form that can cause illness or solve problems

midship: the middle part of a ship

Morse code: a code in which sounds or lights represent each letter in the alphabet

oceanographer: a scientist who studies the oceans

optical illusion: a visual combination of color and light that sends misleading signals to our brains

porthole: a small window on a ship or airplane

pound: a unit of British money

radius: the measurement of a circle or sphere

reciprocal engine: an engine that turns pressure, such as the pressure from rising steam, into motion

rivet: a metal pin used to hold sheets of metal together

riveter: a person who receives a hot rivet and pounds it into place

salvage: to rescue or remove an object from a shipwreck

shipyard: a place where ships are built or repaired

slipway: a boat ramp used to move a ship from land to water

sonar: the bouncing back of sound waves, used in the air or the water to find things

soot: black powder produced when burning coal and other materials

starboard: the right side of a ship when you are facing the bow

stateroom: living quarters on a ship

steerage: the least expensive passenger section of an ocean liner

stern: the back of a ship

steward: a person whose job is taking care of passengers on a ship or airplane

stoker: a man who loaded coal into furnaces

stopwatch: a watch used to measure or time the duration of an activity

submersible: a research submarine that can travel in deep water

supermoon: a moon that seems especially large and has an added gravitational pull because it's closer to Earth than usual

telepresence: visual contact without being close by

throttle: a device that controls the flow of fuel to an engine

transatlantic: crossing the Atlantic Ocean

tripe: the stomach of an animal such as a cow, used for food

turbine: a machine with a wheel or blades that spin when steam, water, or air flows through them

watertight: constructed tightly so that water can't get in or out

wrought iron: iron with very little carbon

REFERENCES

BOOKS AND ARTICLES

Blum, Sam. "The Hunt for the Titanic Was Actually a Hunt for Lost U.S. Nuclear Submarines." *Popular Mechanics*, December 17, 2018. popularmechanics.com/military/navy-ships/a25603601/titanic-discovery-nuclear-submarines-navy.

Bryant, Kelly. "What Life Was Like Aboard the Titanic." *Reader's Digest*, March 21, 2019. rd.com/culture/what-life-was-like-aboard-the-titanic.

Clarke, Jim. "Titanic Disaster: How History Has Judged Bolton's Sea Captains." BBC News, April 11, 2012. bbc.com/news/uk-england-manchester-17678822.

Cohen, Jennie. "Titanic's First Victim Gets Headstone at Last." History.com, A&E Television Networks, August 2, 2011. history.com/news/titanics-first-victim-gets-headstone-at-last.

Coltman, Richard. "Downshire House; London." Titanic Memorials.co.uk, June 14, 2013. titanicmemorials.co.uk/post/memorial/downshire+house+london.

Cox, Frank. "The Titanic's First Victim." Encyclopedia Titanica, May 15, 2012. encyclopedia-titanica.org/the-titanics-first-victim.html.

Daugherty, Greg. "Here's What the Most Expensive Ticket on the Titanic Would Have Bought You." *Money*, April 14, 2016. money.com/titanic-most-expensive-ticket.

Deutsche Welle. "Submarine Trip to the Titanic Booking Soon—for Those with Deep Pockets." DW.com, September 1, 2019. dw.com/en/submarine-trip-to-the-titanic-booking-soon-for-those-with-deep-pockets/a-47001755.

Discover Northern Ireland. "Titanic Sailing Route Map." Tourism Northern Ireland, 2020. discovernorthernireland.com/things -to-do/attractions/titanic/titanic-sailing-route-map.

Eschner, Kat. "The Chief Designer of the 'Titanic' Saved Everyone He Could as His Ship Went Down." *Smithsonian Magazine*, February 7, 2017. smithsonianmag.com/smart-news/chief -designer-titanic-saved-everyone-he-could-his-ship-went -down-180962008.

Garber, Megan. "The Technology That Allowed the Titanic Survivors to Survive." *Atlantic*, April 13, 2012. theatlantic.com /technology/archive/2012/04/the-technology-that-allowed -the-titanic-survivors-to-survive/255848.

Greshko, Michael. "Titanic Artifacts Caught in International Tug-of-War." *National Geographic*, July 2, 2018. national geographic.com/science/2018/07/news-rms-titanic-artifacts -shipwrecks-bankruptcy-archaeology.

Handwerk, Brian. "Paint the Titanic, Wreck's Discoverer Says." *National Geographic*, April 12, 2012. nationalgeographic .com/news/2012/4/120412-titanic-100-anniversary-paint -ballard-science.

History Press. "Building Titanic." 2020. thehistorypress.co.uk /titanic/building-titanic.

_____. "How Was the Wreck of the Titanic Discovered?" 2020. thehistorypress.co.uk/articles/how-was-the-wreck-of-the -titanic-discovered.

IrishCentral. "Titanic Struck an Iceberg After Receiving Seven Warnings." April 14, 2020. irishcentral.com/news/titanic -struck-iceberg-warnings.

Knjazmilos. "The Ice Warnings Received by Titanic." Titanic -Titanic.com, June 17, 2019. titanic-titanic.com/the-ice -warnings-received-by-titanic.

Kozupsky, Jordana. "Jeremiah Burke Sent Message in a Bottle from the Titanic." IrishCentral, April 5, 2020. irishcentral .com/roots/history/jeremiah-burke-message-bottle-titanic.

Lewis, Danny. "A Coal Fire May Have Helped Sink the 'Titanic.'" *Smithsonian Magazine*, January 5, 2017. smithsonianmag .com/smart-news/coal-fire-may-have-helped-sink-titanic -180961699.

Lonergan, Aidan. "Thomas Andrews: Seven Facts About the Irishman Who Designed the Titanic and Went Down with His Ship." *Irish Post*, February 7, 2017. irishpost.com/life-style /thomas-andrews-seven-facts-irishman-designed-titanic -went-ship-113110.

Lovett, Richard. "Titanic Sunk by 'Supermoon' and Celestial Alignment?" *National Geographic*, March 6, 2012. nationalgeographic.com/news/2012/3/120306-titanic -supermoon-moon-science-iceberg-sky-sink.

Lynch, Don. *Titanic*. New York: Hyperion Books, 1998.

Malcomb, Andrea. "Building the Titanic." Molly Brown House Museum, 2020. mollybrown.org/building-the-titanic.

Maritime Executive. "Carpathia's Role in Titanic's Rescue." May 31, 2015. maritime-executive.com/article/carpathias-role -in-titanic-rescue.

Marschall, Ken. *Ken Marschall's Art of the Titanic*. New York: Hyperion Books, 1998.

Marschall, Ken, and Hugh Brewster. *Inside the Titanic*. New York: Little, Brown, 1997.

Matthews, Alex. "Luxurious Life on Titanic Revealed in Rare Brochures." *Daily Mail*, April 5, 2017. dailymail.co.uk/news /article-4383276/Rare-brochures-reveal-luxurious-life -Titanic.html.

Morelle, Rebecca. "Titanic Sub Dive Reveals Parts Are Being Lost to Sea." BBC News, August 21, 2019. bbc.com/news/science-environment-49420935.

National Geographic. "How the Titanic Was Lost and Found." August 22, 2019. nationalgeographic.com/culture/topics/reference/titanic-lost-found.

Ofgang, Erik. "Two Fallen Nuclear Submarines and Their Top-Secret Link to the Titanic." *Connecticut Magazine*, April 17, 2019. connecticutmag.com/history/two-fallen-nuclear-submarines-and-their-top-secret-link-to/article_e51b5b16-129b-11e8-86b4-db81d90a7f9c.html.

Patrick, Colin. "11 Questionable Suggestions for Raising the Titanic." Mental Floss, April 11, 2012. mentalfloss.com/article/30427/11-questionable-suggestions-raising-titanic.

Peek, Jeff. "Titanic Went Down 107 Years Ago Today, Taking a French Luxury Car with It." Hagerty, April 15, 2019. hagerty.com/media/automotive-history/titanic-sinks-with-1912-renault-aboard.

Pierce, Nicola. *Titanic.* Dublin: The O'Brien Press Ltd., 2018.

Planet Science. "Finding the Titanic." planet-science.com/categories/over-11s/technology/2012/04/finding-the-titanic.aspx. Accessed June 17, 2020.

RMS Titanic and Its Passengers. "Titanic Passes Her Sea Trials." February 9, 2012. titanicstory.wordpress.com/2012/02/09/titanic-passes-her-sea-trials.

Rossignol, Ken. *Titanic 1912.* Privateer Clause Publishing: 2012.

Rumble, Robert. "Why Do Ships Have a Gender?" Imperial War Museums, April 24, 2019. iwm.org.uk/history/why-do-ships-have-a-gender.

SciJinks. "What Causes Tides?" National Oceanic and Atmospheric Association, June 16, 2020. scijinks.gov/tides.

Seaward Marine Services LLC. "Underwater Painting."
Seaward-Marine.com, 2020. seaward-marine.com/services
/husbandry/hycote.

Shaw, Gabbi. "Titanic Secrets and Little-Known Facts." Insider,
April 3, 2020. insider.com/titanic-secrets-facts-2018-4.

Simpson, Mark. "Sinking Was Disaster but Ship Was Engineering
Triumph." BBC News, May 31, 2011. bbc.com/news/uk
-northern-ireland-13595400.

Smithsonian Magazine. "Did the Titanic Sink Because of an Optical Illusion?" March 1, 2012. smithsonianmag.com/science
-nature/did-the-titanic-sink-because-of-an-optical-illusion
-102040309.

Thomas Jr., Robert Mcg. "Jack F. Grimm, 72, Is Dead; A Seeker of
Oil and Legends." *New York Times*, January 9, 1998. nytimes
.com/1998/01/09/us/jack-f-grimm-72-is-dead-a-seeker-of
-oil-and-legends.html.

Times Wire Services. "Wreck of Liner Titanic Found: 'Absolutely
Certain,' US-French Team Says." *Los Angeles Times*,
September 3, 1985. latimes.com/archives/la-xpm-1985
-09-03-mn-24236-story.html.

Titanic Historical Society. "Titanic's 'Brittle' Steel?" October 24,
2017. titanichistoricalsociety.org/titanics-brittle-steel.

Triton. "Triton Completes the First Human Occupied Submersible
Dives on Titanic in 14 Years." TritonSubs.com, August 2019.
tritonsubs.com/2019/08/21/triton-completes-the-first-human
-occupied-submersible-dives-on-titanic-in-14-years.

Tsang, Amie. "The Titanic's Artifacts Are About to Change Hands.
Here's What's for Sale." *New York Times*, October 17, 2018.
nytimes.com/2018/10/17/business/titanic-treasures-bids
-hedge-funds.html.

UNESCO. "The Wreck of the Titanic Is Protected by UNESCO from 15 April 2012 Onwards. . . ." UNESCO.org, 2017. unesco.org /new/en/culture/themes/underwater-cultural-heritage/the -heritage/did-you-know/titanic.

United Press International. "Vaseline Can Raise the Titanic." September 9, 1985. upi.com/Archives/1985/09/09/Vaseline -can-raise-the-Titanic/6614495086400.

US Coast Guard Navigation Center. "How Large Was the Iceberg That Sank the Titanic." Department of Homeland Security, June 19, 2009. navcen.uscg.gov/?pageName=iipHowLarge WasTheIcebergThatSankTheTITANIC.

Woods Hole Oceanographic Institution. "Ships & Technology Used During the Titanic Expeditions." WHOI.edu, 2020. whoi.edu /know-your-ocean/ocean-topics/underwater-archaeology /rms-titanic/ships-technology-used-during-the-titanic -expeditions.

Woytowich, Richard. "How Did Titanic Really Break Up?" *Scientific American*, April 9, 2012. blogs.scientificamerican.com /guest-blog/how-did-titanic-really-break-up.

VIDEOS

Ghosts of the Abyss. Walt Disney Pictures, 2003.

Titanic: 100 Year Anniversary. National Geographic, 2012.

Titanic: 20 Years Later with James Cameron. National Geographic, 2017.

Titanic: A Legend Born in Belfast. Network Ireland, 2012.

"Titanic Archive: 1957 Interviews," Edith's interview. BBC South Today, posted April 25, 2012. youtube.com/watch?v =FVLiZo6Pkak.

Titanic Arrogance. Journeyman Pictures, 2011.

Titanic: Band of Courage. TH Entertainment, 2014.

Titanic: In Her Own Words. BBC Radio, 2012.

Titanic Mystery Solved. National Geographic, 2016.

Titanic: The Complete Story. A&E Home Video, 2002.

Titanic: The Final Word with James Cameron. National Geographic, 2012.

Titanic: The History and Maiden Voyage of the Luxury Liner. Top5Media, 2017.

Titanic Words of the Titanic. Posted on YouTube by Korabl'-Legenda Titanik, April 22, 2012. youtube.com/watch?v=KTGLWzuUY7s &feature=emb_logo.

Waking the Titanic. Timeline World History, 2012.

ABOUT THE AUTHOR

 **Kelly Milner Halls** has written nonfiction for young readers for the past 25 years. She has had more than 50 books and 1,000 articles published and plans to write 50 more. Halls makes her home in Spokane, Washington, with her two daughters, a rescue Great Dane named Abbey, and too many rescue cats . . . but who's counting? For more about her, visit wondersofweird.com.